JUST BE

To My dear
friend Corter

Just Be

Addison Palmore

ISBN: 1535142197
ISBN 13: 9781535142199

Dedicated to my teachers

Christ, The Buddha, MSI, Shiva Ishaya, Kali Ishaya, Bhagavati Ishaya, Eckhart Tolle, Tom Sledd, Bob Collins, Peter Foley, and Bill Wilson. Words could not begin to express my gratitude for all of your unconditional love and support.

What I know so far…

In my early 40's I felt like I had a firm grasp on happiness. I had checked all the boxes on my wish list. I had been happily married for 14 years, and my wife and I were business partners. We had recently sold our company, that we started together, to a large corporation, and we were financially secure. I had an active spiritual life, several hobbies that I loved, and felt connected to my community. Life seemed balanced and full. What could possibly go wrong? That question makes me laugh now!

My wife decided that we had had grown apart and asked me for a divorce. This came un-expectantly and I was devastated. I had always believed that marriage was forever. We parted ways amicably and remained friends.

I was left with a giant hole in my heart, and I couldn't get any relief. My so-called happiness had obviously been built on a house of cards. I began recklessly spending money and trying to numb the pain through any distraction possible. I frequently had suicidal thoughts so I tried support groups and therapy. They helped but I still felt utterly alone and broken.

One day, after feeling like this for two years and begging God for relief, I woke up feeling completely different. I ran to the table where I had stacks of paper from songs I had written, and I started writing the strangest things. They didn't seem to be coming from me. At least not the "me" I had always known.

One thing I wrote was that money is not the currency of life, love is. Another was that all of our societal problems are caused by the energy of fear, and they are all solvable. I wrote that we humans are addicted to our own thinking, and we create all of our perceived problems by believing false stories in our minds. That we actually create our own reality one moment at a time.

I wrote that we take ourselves way too seriously! That everything in the universe, including us, is energy in motion. Therefore we can choose for the energy of love, in every moment, and allow life to flow with little or no effort.

I also wrote that there is no distinction between myself and every other living creature of earth. That as I raise my own vibration, I energetically elevate everyone on earth simultaneously. That human beings, nature, God, and the universe are all one thing. Therefore we are only in one relationship. Many more pages of things like this were to follow.

I realized that I had been unconsciously relying on the external substitutes for peace such as relationships, physical comfort, social standing, perceived financial security, accomplishments, and many more. If all of this were stripped away I was left with a deep sense of fear and loneliness.

I had been energetically blocked from the love that had always been within me. I knew that I never again had to "do" anything to experience peace and joy. I could simply be.

That day I realized that everything I ever believed had been untrue, and I felt a sense of relief that I couldn't begin to describe. I was overwhelmed with gratitude for all of my pain and suffering, and saw all of it as a lesson. I felt totally free and connected like when I was a little boy.

I had a real awakening that day which was about a decade ago. Some sort of inner explosion where my brain was suddenly reorganized. Since then I have been on an inner journey to feed my soul, and help others discover what I have found.

Following that awakening I committed to few effortless daily practices with all of the zeal I could summon. I was utterly surprised at how fast stress was leaving my mind and body on a daily basis, while at the same time preventing new stress from coming in. This has proven to be a much better way to live!

Through the ideas and practices outlined in this book I have continually been amazed by the deeper levels of peace and joy a human being can experience. This beautiful energy spreads to others very quickly, and life becomes effortless. I hope you find something useful in these pages. Everything written here has come from my direct experience. Take what you want or need, and leave the rest. I invite you to join me on this beautiful journey and Just Be...

IDEAS

PRACTICES

FORWARD

The pressure is off!

We are totally ok as we are. We do not have to do anything to be ok. We especially do not have to do anything to deserve love. The love within us is our birthright and can never be taken away. Isn't it about time we stop buying in to the collective insanity around us, and start living?

At a subconscious level most things we do, including what we do for others, is in pursuit of gaining a sense of peace or connectedness. We are already connected, and peace is our natural state.

Just being doesn't mean we cease all activity. The act of being is extremely dynamic! We can actually accomplish far more with less effort!

Our destiny is to live a life of meaning and purpose. Living to our full potential, and helping others do the same. A life of inspiration not obligation!

There are two parts to this book. Part one is a collection of ideas that point to the experience of "being". It is suggested that you contemplate these ideas at a relaxed pace.

Part two is a series of specific practices to assist you on your path. Without the practices this book is simply more information. Combining the practices with the information can be extremely powerful.

SUGGESTION

After you finish reading each idea take a few minutes to contemplate what you have read. Effortlessly think the phrase "Thank you for this moment – exactly as it is". Allow your thoughts to pass in front of the blank screen in your mind. Feel your feelings fully.

The word "Thank" will tap you into the higher frequency of gratitude. The word "you" is a placeholder to insert the name of whatever you call your highest force for good. Examples of this are: God, the universe, the source of everything, the energy of love, the stillness, Christ, and many more. You choose.

The word "Moment" refers to anything that can be perceived in this exact moment.

The phrase "Exactly as it is" points toward the full acceptance of now.

As you read the words on each page you are activating the left hemisphere of the brain or the analytical mind. When you take a moment to contemplate gratitude you are drifting into the right hemisphere of the mind which is spacious, loving, and creative.

We create balance by activating both sides of our brain. As we cultivate balance in our mind, our outer world falls into place naturally and effortlessly. We become of maximum benefit to ourselves and the world when we achieve balance. This is our natural state.

Thank you for this moment – exactly as it is

AWE AND WONDER

Can you remember a time in your life when everything around you seemed exciting and fascinating? All of your wants and needs were met in that moment, and you felt a sense of awe and wonder? Time stood still, and life seemed perfect.

Maybe you were on vacation or simply sitting in your back yard listening to the birds. What if I told you that you can experience this level of peace whenever you choose, no matter what you are doing or who you are with. Would you be interested? Would you believe this is even possible?

In order experience this we must stop trying to be happy. When we are trying to be happy we are not happy. The idiom "The struggle is real" is merely a perception. The struggle is in our minds only.

Freedom has nothing to do with our external circum-stances, being a good person or leading an exciting life. It comes from peeling away the internal layers of untruth, and shining the light on what lies behind the curtain.

As we begin to follow our heart in every moment, with single pointed focus, all of our fear drops away. We are left with a sense of well-being far deeper than joy. The only thing keeping us from this is our fear of the unknown.

By embracing uncertainty life becomes quite certain. We allow what is right in front of us to unfold naturally. Our intuition will provide the roadmap. No more trying to figure it out. Total clarity.

When we have a vision in our mind's eye about how we can further benefit the world we live in, an opportunity will present itself out of nowhere. There is full trust that whatever we create in this moment serves our highest good.

We simply need to relax and stop taking ourselves so seriously! The entire human race is spending a fortune on a daily basis to relax. Our natural state is a relaxed state of love. As we travel from our head to our heart the search for happiness ends.

Thank God for this momen – exactly as it is

I AM NOT

We are not our name. Of course we must call ourselves something but this is merely a nametag. We are not our body. We are not our thoughts or feelings. We are not defined by our material possessions or the size of our bank account.

We are not our status in society or accomplishments. We are not what we do for a living. It does not matter where we live. We are not our dreams, aspirations or beliefs.

We are not defined by any relationship including friends and family. We are not our story. The past has nothing to do with us now, and the future is an illusion occurring in our minds right now.

So what are we? We are spirit. We are energy. We are intelligence. We are divine. We are love. We are human. We simply are...

There really isn't any language to describe what we are. The possibilities are endless. This is comforting to know because it removes the pressure to be anything.

Everything in creation breaks down to the same microscopic particles. Space doesn't exist, and it is everything at the same time. Could it be that our soul is directly connected to the source of everything or God?

When we become heart centered the answers to this question and many others become clear. The heart is far more intelligent than the mind.

There is a big difference between understanding this intellectually, and experiencing it first-hand. Living from our heart is the land of milk and honey. There is no judgement of self or anything else in this space. There is only love of self and everything in creation.

From this place we realize that we can literally create a little slice of heaven for ourselves, right here on earth.

Thank the universe of God for this moment...

CHOICES

When we were born we were in our natural state of mind which is loving and peaceful. For a brief time we were living from our hearts. Soon after we adopted worry and expectations of the people around us. This often becomes more intense as the years go by but we are often unaware.

Many began to live a survival based lifestyle like everyone around us. Fear based thought processes were embedded into our minds in the form of belief.

We believe that our bodies should look a certain way or that we should make a certain amount of money. We often believe that there is something wrong with our lives, and that we are limited and totally separate. These fear-based beliefs are untrue, and merely perceptions.

The result of living this way over time has created stress in our minds and bodies that we aren't aware of. This build-up of stress is the root cause of most of our mental and physical discomfort.

We can totally reverse this!

We become free from the inside out. The inside is the eternal light that we are. The outside is our mind, bodies and environment.

Most human suffering starts with lack of acceptance. Confusing the real with the unreal. The permanent from the impermanent. By focusing on love in every moment we transcend our only block to peace. Our thinking.

As we choose for the stillness that lies behind all activity we begin to see the truth which is extremely freeing. We are no longer burdened by shame and guilt. We stop playing the role of a victim, and we no longer feel sorry for ourselves.

We can focus on our highest force for good in every moment. This will dissolve a lot of the fear running in the background that we may not be aware of. Such as the fear of death.

Fear of dying actually prevents us from truly living. Imagine letting go of all of our anxiety around our health, finance, and romance. Embracing life fully.

We can also choose to let go of our desire to be right. We are never right. Everything is perception. We dispute everything from religion to politics. This is exhausting.

Ask yourself this question. What does love look like in any given situation? Simply asking this question will immediately access your intuition. Here you will find truth.

We can choose for the unshakable force of love in every moment. The energy of God or source can always be experienced when we turn our attention to it. As we do this we find that we are no longer working so hard, and life becomes effortless.

Thank the stillness for this moment...

OUR BEAUTIFUL MIND

UNLIMITED

We currently think between 60,000 to 80,000 thoughts per day. Not that long ago we thought half as many thoughts as we do now. We are not any smarter.

Most of our thoughts have nothing to do with reality. We are so consumed with the past and future that we rarely experience the beauty of what is happening right now.

All of our chaos and confusion comes from our thinking. We think we are controlling our thoughts but they are controlling us. Technology is adding to our imbalanced thinking.

Fear based thinking occurs in our left brain which is the analytical part of our mind. Very little of this thinking is based in truth.

Conversely all of our upward directed thinking comes from our heart, which is a direct link to source or God. This thinking is in present time.

When we find ourselves free of thought for a moment we feel a sense of relief. We can see that there really isn't anything going on except in our minds. There is no past or future, only right now.

We cannot utilize our thinking mind to create love or peace. In other words we cannot simply decide to be positive in all situations. It doesn't work like that. This is attempting to use the ego to fix the ego.

Affirmations on the surface of the mind will only provide temporary results, and ultimately cause more discursive thinking.

An example of this is when you are experiencing negative thinking, and you say something positive like "life is wonderful". This doesn't work because it isn't authentic. This thinking is occurring on the surface of the mind where there is zero power.

Once we get beyond the surface of the mind, and into our heart, we can make real progress. Then we can begin to create a tipping point in our consciousness and allow the confusion to dissipate.

Simply take a deep breath and think the phrase "Thank you for this moment —exactly as it is". When you think the words "Thank you", you are talking to your highest force for good such as God or the universe.

Regardless of what is occurring in your life this simple phrase can alter your reality in a positive way.

By focusing on gratitude in this moment the ego will yield every time. This practice will penetrate the surface of the mind, and you will briefly visit to the deepest part of your consciousness.

So by introducing one heart-centered thought in the mix with the other 75,000 thoughts we become more peaceful and content.

This is much like dropping a small pellet of chlorine into a murky swimming pool. The water becomes clear and vibrant within seconds! The more we do this, the less confusion we experience. We begin to live from our heart which will always guide us.

Thank the the grace of God for this moment...

GRAIN OF SALT

What is true?

Words in the dictionary that are associated with the word believe are: imagine, suppose, assume, presume and conclude. There is a big difference in believing in God, and having a direct experience of God.

When we travel from our head to our heart we experience the divine first hand. No need to believe anything.

Anytime we come to a conclusion about anything in our mind and believe it, we are creating a little slice of chaos for ourselves down the road. We all have fixed ideas about ourselves, others, and the world. This is how we think things are. These beliefs are lodged so deeply in our minds, we don't even know they are there. It is all happening at a subconscious level.

We may be getting some fabulous new insight but our underlying beliefs are preventing us from using our new insight. In fact we may be sharing our new insights with others as though we have adopted them into our life. We aren't even aware that this is happening. This is because we are operating from the thinking mind. There is no power in this realm, just more thinking.

We can allow our experience and intuition to pave the road. Some beliefs serve us. Such as a belief in a higher power. However if we believe that we are separate, small or limited we will create that very scenario in our life. Often we aren't aware of our most destructive beliefs.

It is entirely possible to dissolve all of the belief systems our mind. This is like losing a giant ball and chain we have been carrying since childhood. This will take practice and consistency over time. This is the practice of unlearning everything we have ever learned.

We have the ability to discern the truth in any situation. No more confusion. Believing anything is the same as placing limits on it. Remaining open allows for unlimited possibilities.

There are specific practices in the part 2 of the book aimed at penetrating the surface of the mind where all belief is stored. Through practice we can be free from all limited ideas.

Thank the source of everything for this moment ...

INFORMATION OVERLOAD

Our insatiable desire for more information is destroying our collective spirit. We are drowning in an ocean of content which is being confused with truth.

We could read the best book ever written on unconditional love, and still have little idea how to actually love unconditionally. When we are able to tap into heart centered awareness, we clearly see what we have always known.

The answers to everything that could ever be known can only be found in this moment. Letting go of the needing to know answers in the form of information is extremely freeing.

The unknown is known

Awareness is far more intelligent than information, especially in matters of the heart. This is when we have a moment free of thought, and we feel a sense of understanding and connection.

In such a moment we are at peace, and feel completely connected to everyone and everything. In that moment, by not knowing, we know everything.

It is easy to get caught in the trap of confusing information with true knowing. Doesn't it feel great to throw your hands in the air and simply say "I don't know"? It feels good for a reason!

Thank the holy-spirit for this moment...

LIFELONG IMPRESSIONS

We all have boundless potential however many of us have difficulty reaching our potential due to negative impressions imbedded in our cellular memory.

For many of us some of the following stressful emotions or states of mind are lurking just beneath the surface; fear, discontentment, anxiety, worry, anger, shame, guilt, sense of betrayal or abandonment, sense of entitlement, and victim mentality. By focusing on these deep seeded grooves we are blocked from the sunlight of the spirit.

Sometimes we need to allow ourselves to completely fall apart emotionally in order to heal. Simply by taking the appropriate alone time each day to be completely quiet and still, and allowing our thoughts and feelings to express themselves, lifelong impressions begin to diminish and stress dissolves! At first this can be extremely uncomfortable and requires commitment. After a while it can become blissful.

By simply focusing on the energy of love we begin to channel the energy of God through our body. The feeling of divine presence is indescribable.

Once we dissolve past impressions, stress and fear melt away. We no longer attach to unhealthy behaviors, people or situations. Life becomes peaceful.

Thank the energy of love for this moment...

LOVE ENERGY

Love is the energy of creation, and the most contagious force in the universe. When we are truly at peace for a moment we have accessed the energy of love. This allows us to energetically affect others with our presence alone. Nothing can compete with the power of love. It is absolute.

The birth of stress

When we consciously or subconsciously experience fear we feel disconnected from source or God. Feelings aren't facts. We are actually never disconnected from source. Fear isn't bad or wrong. It is simply an energy that reacts adversely to love.

The collision between love and fear creates a conflicting thought stream which could be called duality or confusion.

Love is the more powerful of the two energies. Love unites, fear separates. What you feed you breed.

Thoughts and feelings have no meaning until our ego assigns meaning to them. This is where it has gotten tricky for us.

The ego assigns meaning to everything in an attempt to make sense out of our lives. After we assign meaning we actually believe the new meaning as truth. This meaning has no basis in truth it is merely our perception. Like everything else.

This is why time doesn't exist and it is always now. We assigned meaning to the energy in motion and invented the concept of time to create a false sense of order.

When we are able to focus on the energy of love or God exclusively life becomes magical. We become the butterfly. We are no longer trying to become the butterfly.

That is why the title of this book is Just Be. We are no longer doing much of anything. The energy of creation is doing everything through us. Through the practices of stillness and continually facing our fear, we are able to cut through the dense ego mind and discover our true self.

When this happens we are living in a completely different dimension. Our focus shifts from the outside to the inside.

With this razor sharp focus we find ourselves having the courage to look deep-within, and allow life to unfold naturally. We discover who and what we really are.

Thank the source of everything for this moment...

SENSORY ILLUSION

Nothing is as it appears to be. What we are able to decipher through the lens of our five senses is extremely limiting. We are only able to perceive a fraction of reality through our senses. Everything is energy.

Although we can experience this energy, we cannot see, touch, smell, or taste it. Nonetheless we are still prone to believe what we perceive through our senses.

This energy has no agenda as far as humans go. It doesn't care what we do. Like all energy it will react to other energies that it comes into contact with.

Our senses lull us into an illusion that our physical bodies need pleasure, comfort, security, and control. This is a response to stress or fear.

Once we become aware of this we can choose the opposite. We can choose the unknown and put immediate gratification on hold. This includes emotional gratification.

Through daily practice we can cultivate a spacious existence. We can create new neuropathways of love in our brain while cleaning out all of our fear based beliefs from the past. This isn't difficult. It is simply practice.

Thank God energy for this moment...

OPEN YOUR HEART

Humility

There is constant truth that lies beyond all human experience which can be accessed through being totally open and vulnerable in any given moment. This is our ticket to heaven on earth.

The key to feeling connected to our loved ones and our fellow man is opening our hearts. To be vulnerable is to be strong. Opening our heart and let our true self be seen is extremely empowering.

We can express our feelings without any filter. We no longer need to protect our heart! No-one can hurt us unless we allow them to.

When we protect our heart we create separation between ourselves and others. We all need each other. No-one can do this alone.

Imagine a time when you have been upset. If someone were to place a two week old baby in your arms at that exact moment you might not be as upset as you were. The baby is in a pure state of vulnerability. This has the ability to diffuse any emotion.

We all began our lives with pure and open hearts, then many of us began protecting ourselves. Over time we found ourselves in a continual state of protection. When we close our heart we are blocked from the sunlight of the spirit.

Being truly vulnerable is to feel and express our feelings, FULLY. Feelings are the river of life. If we are angry we don't need to act like we are not. If we are sad, we can feel the sadness deeply in the moment.

We don't need to put on a happy face when we are sad, this can be very destructive. Just because we feel a negative emotion doesn't mean that there is anything wrong. It is simply energy moving. If we are excited we get to act exited!

There is no need to use humor or sarcasm to cover up for our true feelings. If we feel insecure, great! Embrace our insecurity. We can embrace whatever is happening inside of us. We can allow all of our emotions to move through us, and be who we really are.

It takes practice to be able to express our true self. We may have to push through some social fear at first, and this can be very uncomfortable.

We can become comfortable being uncomfortable, and let go of our fear of being hurt or embarrassed. Protecting ourselves doesn't always serve our highest good. Being vulnerable will most often serve us.

Deep down we falsely believe that if we really let go and simply be ourselves, that we won't get what we want and need or that we will be hurt. The opposite is true.

Thank God for this moment...

ABSORBING EMOTION

Energy flow from one to another

As we begin to open our hearts and minds we often become more empathetic. This is beautiful because we actually feel what others are feeling which allows us to become more connected and serve.

We may walk into a crowded restaurant and pick up on the energy of someone who is sad without having any interaction with that person. We may also pick up positive energy as well. It is very helpful to be aware of this.

As we clear out our own stress and past impressions we often feel the energy of the collective. When this happens we may assume that we are being overly emotional for some subconscious personal reason. This often isn't the case.

Living life with a wide open heart is like living in another world. Energy spreads very quickly and easily from one person to the next. It is helpful to be mindful of this. Sometimes we need a little break from each-other.

Empathetic souls can be magnets for needy or lonely people. We often want to be available for people in these situations. As we choose for love and gratitude in every moment we are able to maintain our energy levels more easily.

Thank the stillness for this moment...

REMOVE YOUR MASK

Are you able to be truly authentic all day every day? Do you hide behind your happy face at home, school or work? Do you laugh at things that aren't funny just to get along? Do you go along with things that you do not agree with?

Do you actually become a different person depending, on your circumstances or who you are around? This different person is your shadow self. Your mind literally created this other person to survive. We have all experienced the shadow self.

Many people live their entire lives with this mask on. They seldom even come into contact with their true self. Sometimes these people are very successful in many parts of their life but they seldom experience peace.

The shadow self is much like a parasite. Constantly eating away at our ability to love ourselves and others. This can be a difficult way to live.

Finding out who we are and tapping into our true-self is where we find happiness. We can make a choice to act authentically in every moment. We can practice remaining in the stillness even when we are among people. This may be extremely uncomfortable at first.

We can practice not filling the silence with idle conversation. Not laughing at something that isn't funny. Speaking our truth with no filter even when we don't agree. Allow ourselves to act tired when we are tired.

This is true bravery in the face of an uncertain outcome. We begin to stop trying to control every detail in our lives, and allow the chips to fall where they may.

When we begin to live authentically our outside circumstances will line up to support that. We may no longer stay in an unhealthy relationship or job. We may actually trade some external comfort for internal peace. This is always a wise trade.

Thank the universe for this moment...

NOTICE THE LABELS

Good, bad, right, wrong and fine

It is merely our perception that something is right or wrong, good or bad. These categorizations are constantly happening in our daily internal dialog.

Our society labels and judges everything from our bodies to our spiritual enlightenment. Our minds are on auto pilot placing everything in defined categories. This is exhausting.

We can choose differently

Instead of living a miserable relative existence we can choose a life based in truth. The truth is the truth. It cannot be altered, bent or manipulated.

When we tell someone that something is bad we make it even more undesirable. What if we said it was interesting? This may actually make us smile. Choosing different language can alter our reality in the moment.

Every time we observe our mind labelling something as good bad or otherwise we can think the phrase "thank you for this moment -exactly as it is". This practice will stop our ego in its tracks and allow us to see clearly.

The ego attempts to label everything and places into a nice tidy box. This is living a relative existence instead of a life based in truth. Truth can be illuminated in every situation.

Thank you for this moment – exactly as it is

NO MATTER WHAT

Two of the biggest lies we tell ourselves is that "more is better" and "if only things were different". When we place conditions on our happiness we cause suffering for ourselves and others.

By not holding our lives to comparisons we win the lottery of life. We begin to accept whatever is occurring in this moment. No matter what.

We are a complete. We don't need anything to change in this moment to be satisfied. We don't need that special someone to love us any more than they already do. We don't need more of anything to experience peace.

Our mind will make up stories that something is wrong with our body, environment or life. There is nothing wrong. Our life may be uncomfortable at times but that doesn't make it wrong or bad.

By attempting to control people, places and things in order to feel safe, secure, and comfortable, we completely miss the mark and deplete all of our energy. By consistently focusing on gratitude for our life, as it is in this moment, we discover an unshakable sense of peace. Only then will our outer world fall into place.

Thank the source of everything for this moment...

THE ACCLAIM OF MAN

If we seek the acclaim of man we are limited to the acclaim of man. This is a one way ticket to unhappiness. We do not need their approval!

We compare our jobs, relationships, our appearance, bank accounts, spiritual practices, religions, and thousands of others things. This is occurring in our thinking only. As soon as we think we are free of this our ego is doing it in another area of our life.

Creating space in our thinking allows us to experience moments without comparing of judging. This feels fantastic, and we automatically want more.

Our minds are geared to desire the truth and simplicity. So when we treat our mind to a break from constant thought it is pleased.

Gratitude in the moment is an extremely powerful practice to overcome our constant concern about the opinion of others.

It really doesn't matter what anyone thinks! Millions of people pay lip service to this concept every day. Few actually experience it.

As long as we are concerned with others opinions we are completely blocked from becoming who we are meant to be.

Thank you for this moment – exactly as it is

UNCONDITIONAL LOVE

We are love

Unconditional love is accepting someone exactly as they are. Allowing them to be who they are with no editing. It is impossible to truly love another if we do not accept ourselves exactly as we are.

Creating a connection from one enlivened heart to another can only occur when there is no ulterior motive. If we are blocked from the love within, we will demand it from others. When we do not accept ourselves exactly as we are we are taking, not loving.

Being truly selfless is our highest calling but ironically it is by first being selfish that we become selfless. We must actively love ourselves first with no apology. Then we can serve others while expecting nothing in return. This creates a win-win scenario for everyone.

Listening so someone intently is love. Giving up our time for someone is love. Remaining open and letting go of our need to be right is love. Giving someone personal space is an indication of love. Not judging someone is love. Not having expectations is actively loving someone.

Many people confuse the yearning and desiring to be near someone as love. This is closer to attachment than love. Unconditional love is free and detached.

When we do not have an attachment to the outcome or keep track of our good deeds it is love. This is only possible when we are unblocked.

Love is a direct extension of the human heart. It is steeped in acceptance of this moment and the joy of now. One of my favorite definitions of love is the full acceptance of "what is" in this moment.

Any action that would aid you or another into the fullest experience of this moment would be an act of pure love.

Another definition of love is "Unconditional concern for everyone's best interest." This includes our own best interest. Real love is so much bigger than all of our personal relationships.

Love has nothing to do with sex or wedding dresses. Any time there is a condition placed on love it is no longer love. Love never has an agenda. Love can only be experienced in the now.

Are you willing to disappoint another to be true to yourself? This an act of unconditional love even though it may not feel like it. Love seldom feels like we think it should.

Unconditional love is how we could eventually create an enlightened society. A society where we are totally united, and every person is dedicated to the highest good of everyone.

Thank the grace of God for this moment...

RELATIONSHIP

One relationship

Relationship has been the most difficult area of my life. As a child, due to gross neglect and abandonment, I found it very difficult to connect with people. I felt completely unloved, and even worse, unlovable. I also felt like it was my fault that I was unlovable which created a strong sense of shame. This leaked into every area of my life especially relationships.

As I write this chapter I feel compassion for the little boy inside of me that had to go through that. I am eternally grateful that I allowed myself the time and space to truly feel the hurt, anger, and sadness that was trapped inside me for years.

These trapped emotions were actually negative energy that needed to move. The only way for the energy to move was for me to slow down long enough to lean into the uncomfortable feelings. This has allowed me to overcome my conditioning.

As I was moving the trapped emotion out of my nervous system through focused mediation, I began to experience pure love coming from within me. This love was infinitely stronger than anything I had ever experienced.

I realized that love doesn't come from other people. Love is actually what we are! I cried tears of joy for days upon this realization, I had always believed that God is the love from

37

within, and I thought I had experienced it but this was different. For the first time I knew that I could experience this love permanently with no separation.

Now when I form new relationships, I do so with an open trusting heart, and subsequently attract people into my life that are healthy. Toxic and unhealthy people have naturally exited my life with little or no effort. I simply focus on love or God and allow my life unfold. No big deal.

Through the awakening I had many years ago, many hours of daily meditation, and countless hours of working with others to help them heal themselves, I realized that the only relationship we are ever in is the relationship with ourselves.

Every relationship is filtered through our perception and nervous system which means we are literally having a relationship with a perception of someone that is coming from within us. When our buttons are pushed by someone it is our job to remove those buttons, not try to change the other person.

By effortlessly choosing for the energy of love or God in every moment, not on fixing any particular relationship, the buttons dissolve naturally.

It is my experience that we are only in one relationship. The universe is an outward light projection coming from within you or us. That means that God or the energy of creation is everything, including you. When you are in relationship with someone you are looking at God and in the mirror at the same time.

We are in relationship with everything in creation right now. Only an ego would separate out one person or a small group of people and make them special or different. This is what our collective ego has done.

The ego does the same thing when it comes to romantic relationships. Consciousness is looking to expand so the ego is attracted to people that have something we think we want or need. This isn't love it is attachment.

We quickly learn that the other person cannot provide the thing we want or need and we become frustrated. This frustration presents a perfect opportunity to grow.

If we are awake enough to realize that growing in un-conditional love is what we are actually looking for, and our partner is on the same path, we can grow together far more quickly than we could by ourselves. If either party is resistant there will be more suffering unless we part ways or surrender to each other. Surrender is when we fully accept someone exactly as they are.

When there are two willing participants who are indi-vidually focused on real love, with no unhealthy attachment to the other, their ability to truly love each other skyrockets. This type of relationship is where two people become one. This is often referred to as a holistic relationship. They live in joy and service to each other and the world. They become the icing on each other's cake!

Thank the energy of love for this moment...

ENERGY ZAPPERS

There is no mystery why hundreds of television shows and movies have been written about vampires over the years. This phenomenon is happening all around us.

The dynamic in play is the currency of someone's attention. This works the same as all other currencies including money. Supply and demand. If I capture your attention, you will be "paying" attention to me. If my vibration is low, this will make me feel more alive temporally. I will be receiving energy in the form of your undivided attention. This is taking not loving. We do this consciously and unconsciously when we are in fear or feeling emotionally needy, lonely, angry or resentful.

The energy I am speaking of is our life force. It is the love within us that we need to function in our everyday lives.

Below are some methods we use to steal energy from each-other

- Complaining

- Dressing provocative, or flamboyantly

- Being emotionally needy

- Bragging

- Being an overbearing or overly cautious parent. We are stealing energy from our child when we do this.

- Posting excessive content on social media

- Telling long winded stories

- Being passive aggressive

- Making plans for others

- Guilt tripping

- Being contentious, argumentative or self-centered

- Pouting

- Being controlling

- Having unrealistic expectations

The idea is to raise our vibration so that we don't want or need to drain anyone else's energy. Once we do this we will not allow anyone to drain ours.

There is a hedonic set point in the mind when one person is seeking attention from another. Neuropathways are created around oxytocin and dopamine. When these neuro-bands get strong enough from getting that wonderful feeling of receiving attention from another, the brain begins to value the experience as much as food or water. Oxytocin creates comfort and dopamine creates euphoria. This feeling is often confused with love but it is not.

Draining each-others energy is caused by our belief in separation. This false belief creates subconscious fears that we are small and alone. Love comes from within not the other way around.

We are not separate. We can actually experience unity when we effortlessly focus on love and gratitude and love throughout our day. If you find yourself being zapped or zapping someone else choose for the phrase below. Love and gratitude have the power to stop this in its tracks.

Thank the energy of love for this moment…

PERSONAL CONTRACTS

People in our lives usually aren't there for the reasons we think. This includes family members, friends or spouses. Our souls have made contracts with each person in our life to allow us to expand. The more contrast they present to us the more we expand.

When a particular person is driving us crazy they are teaching us more than anyone! Every person in our path can teach us something. We are living in a giant classroom.

We always have permission to alter the nature of any relationship. Relationships never end, they simply change form. We get to create what types of relationship to have with someone.

Thank the stillness for this moment...

WE ARE NEVER ALONE

A deep sense of loneliness has nothing to do with not being around people or not having a strong family system. It has nothing to do with being in or out of a relationship. It has everything to do with our false belief in separation. We think we are alone therefore we are.

Loneliness is a dis-ease or a state of being uneasy. The mind simply perceives that we are separate, unwanted and alone. When we choose to believe this untrue perception we feel isolated. This is merely blocked energy nothing more.

How can we reconnect when we feel lonely? The state of being lonely is merely a feeling, and it will always pass. We are not our thoughts or our feelings. By embracing our loneliness in the moment we begin to see it for what it is.

Often an event such as a death in the family or a breakup triggers a desperate feeling of loneliness. Of course there is a natural grieving process with any loss but the additional suffering is a choice. We often run from our loneliness through busy activity. This only serves to prolong our agony.

We are all connected to each other and God through our hearts. It is actually impossible to be truly alone. The quickest way to get over the feeling of loneliness is to simply feel it and allow it to run its course.

Spending more time in silent contemplation we allow the blocked energy to move more quickly. Setting aside an entire day alone once a week can completely eliminate the feeling of loneliness.

A day spent completely alone with no cellphones or internet is a gift to ourselves. This is how we can move the fear based energy out of our system.

It is a great day when we finally realize once and for all that we are never alone! From here we can spread this truth. By teaching others that they are their own best friend, we can make a dent in our collective belief in separation.

Thank the universe for this moment...

DESIRE

Desire is part of the human package. In fact the entire universe is constantly expanding through desire. It is always wise to replace judgment with compassion regarding our own desire and the desire of others. Desires must be acknowledged either by letting them go completely or allowing them to run their course.

Underneath it all what we want most is peace and a sense of connectedness. This core desire is often buried underneath a million other desires that make us feel good now. Trying to contain any desire is much like trying to hold onto water by clenching your fist. It's virtually impossible. However, through heart centered practice, your desires will shift to be more in line with your best interest. The heart knows!

Desire from our heart is based in love, and will ultimately serve ourselves and others. Desires based in fear separate us and create chaos. Any desire that strokes our ego or provides immediate gratification is a fear based desire.

Conversely anything that expands our consciousness and allows us to serve others is based in love. We get to choose!

As we reduce the stress in our mind and body by choosing gratitude and love in each moment, we automatically desire less what doesn't serve. Nature is always working in our favor to help us realize our desires.

The state of wanting that which doesn't serve our best interest can be a bottomless pit. These types of desires are usually an attempt to block fear or alleviate anxiety. This can include desire for excessive material accumulation, approval seeking, seeking comfort or security, or sexual fulfillment. There is nothing wrong with any of that! However many of those desires will ultimately cause suffering.

With any desire we can either choose to fulfill it or let it go. When we allow any fear based desire to pass, in lieu of further expansion, we are able to experience truth. The ego wants satisfaction which it can never have. Awareness isn't looking for satisfaction, it simply is.

From a place of awareness we cannot be manipulated or have any desire manipulate others. Once we have tasted true peace of mind our greatest desire will be to further our expansion.

By letting go of every thought we are momentarily free of wanting. As we feel our feelings fully they will pass. We are left with an unlimited blank canvas with which to create. A moment without desire is a moment of freedom.

This process is often called raising our vibration because as we practice this way of life we literally idle at a higher frequency. We feel positive energy flowing through our being.

The irony of this way of life is that many of our previous desires for financial freedom and romance will actually manifest but they no-longer have the same urgency.

Abundance occurs on the inside first and has been with us all along. Desires will come and go. We do not give them power we once did.

This way of life is effortless. We simply focus on love, and gratitude. We are no longer trying gain anything. We simply are…

Thank the stillness for this moment…

ANTICIPATION

Can you remember a time when you were not anticipating the next moment? Maybe after a really tough workout or during a warm bubble bath. Remember how completely satisfied and peaceful you were briefly?

The presence of anticipation can be very agitating. We are often in a mild state of this agitation most of the time. We are constantly anticipating the next moment. This even applies when we are anticipating something pleasant.

One of the reasons we seek pleasure is because it relieves us of anticipation for a short period. This is why ice cream taste so darn good. As soon as we put something sweet in our mouth we aren't anticipating anything. That is why we want more!

The stress we are carrying in our minds and bodies is what is causing us to crave the next moment, and the next one after that. Many of us have gotten so used to living this way we aren't even aware of that it is occurring. As we move the stress out of our bodies we no longer anticipate future events positively or negatively. Life becomes peaceful and we are able to enjoy each moment.

As we observe our mind anticipating something we can think the phrase "thank you for this moment". This will bring the mind back to center for now. Then when the mind begins to anticipate again we simply think "thank you for this moment" again. Eventually the mind begins to slow down.

EXPECTATION

Should've, would've, could've

The society we live in is full of expectation, and it is eating away at our collective soul. This is the opposite of "allowing". Expectation of any kind is a fear-based attempt to control outcomes. When we focus on gratitude in the moment we naturally begin to let go of expectations. We actually receive everything we want and need through letting go of all expectation!

It is a very healthy practice to eliminate the words "should have, would have, and could have" from your speech. These phrases support expectation, and keep us in the lie.

The lie is that something is wrong if it doesn't go the way we wanted it to. It is only our perception that something is wrong. Having expectations of any kind allows us to play the victim. This inevitably strips us of our personal power in the moment.

How can we be free of expectation? Instead of focusing on not having expectations, we simply begin to observe our thinking. We can actually watch as our minds are doing this.

It is the opposite of love to place expectations on ourselves or others. There is a big difference between asking and expecting. We can ask for anything, and then let go of the result.

Thank the energy of love for this moment...

ATTACHMENT

The opposite of "Being"

Often by seeking pleasure we create suffering. Our ego is always looking for something to fixate on to keep us from truly feeling our feelings. Running from one attachment to the next, and never stopping to smell the roses.

This isn't living it is existing

We do not actually need to give up anything to be free. We do however need to be willing to give up everything.

Especially any person, place, behavior, material possession, thought stream or belief that is blocking us from experiencing the love within. Willingness is the key.

We become attached to our own drama, emotional pain, toxic relationships, power from sex or money, physical pain, food, drugs, alcohol, television, internet, certain people, receiving attention, illusion of control, greed, spiritual practices, religion, political views, dieting, material- possessions, laziness, being intelligent, exercise, our appearance, being happy, the past, the future, and being right. Most of all we become attached to our own beliefs.

We often receive emotional payoffs by playing the victim and perpetuating this suffering. We are seldom aware of this as it is occurring.

Judgement makes it worse. To the ego there is no difference between being attached to illegal drugs or to spiritual practice that isn't working anymore. When we are attached to anything we suffer.

Attachment is merely blocked energy – NO BIG DEAL

When we try to break free from an attachment it often gets stronger. The ego is very threatened by this, and will hang on for dear life.

Attachments and addictions often disappear, then manifest in another destructive behavior at a later time. We must get to the root cause, and move the blocked-energy. We cannot simply change our behavior, and expect anything to really shift.

We can replace our attachment with something that works. By introducing some quiet meditation in our day, we can spend time out of our cognitive, and sensory mind. We will begin to detox from the dopamine and serotonin influx from many of these attachments. This enables us to stay present, and embrace being uncomfortable.

We can make being uncomfortable a game that we play in our mind. Before long being uncomfortable feels pleasant because we know that we are loving ourselves. Then eventually it is no longer uncomfortable.

We can physically improve our brain. As we abstain from the behavior and replace it with something healthy, we literally change the chemistry in our mind. Neuropathways of real love are created as the attachment pathway's dissolve.

Thank you for this moment – exactly as it is
58

SPOTTING OUR AGENDAS

Doing to get…

Our society has formed a grid around millions of little fear based exchanges disguised as love. I will scratch your back if you scratch mine. Unfortunately we have adopted this philosophy for everything including matters of the heart. **We do not ever have to do anything to deserve the love that has always been within us!** We often lose sight of this in our daily lives. The best of us are often running agendas that we are not aware of in order to feel worthy, and society applauds us for it.

Do you beat yourself up for small things like forgetting someone's birthday or your own wedding anniversary? Do you hold yourself to standards that you would never expect from others? Do you feel like you have to go to every funeral or every wedding? Do feel like you have to answer the phone when it rings or return every text and email? Are you constantly in service to others while at the same time depleting your own life force?

Have you ever blamed or judged others for not reciprocating? If you say yes to these type of questions you may be unaware that you have an unconscious agenda to get the love that has always been within you by being a good person or pleasing people. This isn't love and we have all done it! Never beat yourself up!

Do you pray to God or the universe to influence the outcomes of situations in your life because you are afraid? Such as healing a person that you are afraid to lose. Do you meditate and practice mindfulness in order to manifest romance, health and wealth?

Whenever we are doing anything to get something we are missing the mark. When we do this we are taking, not loving or serving. Maybe we are in a job that we dislike for a paycheck only. If we redirect our purpose from simply receiving a paycheck to spreading love and kindness while we are at work, expecting nothing in return, our entire life will improve and we will still get a paycheck.

Manifestations only occur when we completely let go of expectation. Everything is energy. It never actually matters much what we are doing. It totally matters why we are doing it!

This is where the human ego becomes the great imposter! The ego can actually mimic real love and it is extremely believable. A person could go an entire lifetime doing good works and saintly deeds and never become free on the inside. You may say "well that's ok at least they helped a lot of people" but this isn't necessarily true. We cannot transmit what we don't have.

There is a much better way for us to live! Through briefly transcending our conditioned mind throughout the day we begin to see the world as it is. The **real** world, where there is peace and harmony, exist beyond the thinking mind illusion that we have created for ourselves. This beautiful place coexist with the 3d existence that many of us have experienced most of our lives. It is our choice as to which world we want to live in!

Thank God for this moment – exactly as it is

OVER IDENTIFICATION

What would you say if a random stranger asked you who and what you are? Would you tell them what you do for a living or that you are a parent. Would you tell them the name of a particular religion you belong to? Do you see the world a certain way because you suffer from physical pain, depression or attention deficit disorder?

Our egos are always looking to categorize and place labels on everything about us. These labels become beliefs, and a source of further suffering. None of these labels are based in truth they are simply mind created attachments.

This can be very tricky because we may transcend being identified with one label only to find out later that our ego has latched on to something else. An example of this would be someone who is over- identified with being a jogger.

This person tells everyone that they meet that they are a jogger. All of the clothes they wear are jogging related. All of the people they associate with are joggers or admirers of joggers. As the years go by they win many awards, and get written up in the newspaper for their success. Perhaps they even marry a fellow jogger and start a little jogging family.

Then one day while jogging in the rain they step in a small pot hole and break their ankle in five pieces. The doctor tells them that their jogging days are over. They are devastated and they don't know who they are anymore.

Soon after someone tells them of a support group for ex-joggers. Reluctantly they attend several of the meetings and immediately find a connection. Through discussing their attachment to jogging with other ex-joggers they find meaning and purpose.

They begin telling everyone about their new support group. They have T-shirts made with the name of their jogging support group on the front. Everyone they associate with is either a member of the support group or a possible member. They spend so much time and energy with their support group, there is little time for anything else.

Before long this starts causing issues with their family, and affecting their life in other areas. They start to feel superior to others because they are an expert on jogging, and recovering from jogging. This arrogance begins to create separation between themselves and others. They realize that they have become bitter and unhappy all over again.

After some soul searching they realize that they had merely switched from one attachment to another, and had never addressed the root cause of all attachment which is being identified with their thinking.

We see over-identification with doctors, lawyers, athletes, therapist, preachers, business leaders, politicians, parents, spiritual leaders, entertainers, 12 step gurus, and yogis who have become over-identified with their practice and dogma. The ego is extremely tricky! It will always re-build itself and come from a completely different angle.

Over-identification comes from our thinking mind. Once we begin to observe our thinking we can create balance, and see this coming before we get attached. This is extremely freeing.

It can be difficult do this alone. We often need people that we trust in our lives to tell us when we are off track. Preferably those who are on a similar path, and know the common pitfalls of an inner journey.

Thank the Holy Spirit for this moment…

REAL COURAGE

We are truly courageous when we can lean into our fear. The only way to transcend fear is to feel it and accept it for what it is. Fear is harmless. It can only harm us if we react to it.

We can choose to be courageous by facing our fear, and using it as a spiritual practice. This can be uncomfortable at first.

Most fear comes from taking something from the past and placing it into the future. This is a complete fantasy but we believe it at the time.

We create anxiety by thinking that we need to solve this fantasy problem in the future, and at the same time solve all of our current perceived problems now. This is merely a false perception and totally insane.

Most of us have certain fears that have come up in our lives over and over. It could be social fear, financial fear, relationship issues, fear of abandonment, and many others.

These fears often lead to health problems such as emotional pain, physical pain, disease, addiction, and a myriad of other issues. We create all of these issues with our internal stress and fear.

The great news is that we can choose to use these issues as our sole catalyst for spiritual growth. We can view our perceived weaknesses as our greatest gift.

By choosing love and gratitude in every moment we begin to see where the fear is coming from and that it cannot harm us. . Then instead of running from it through some activity, substance, or behavior, we simply embrace it exactly as it is.

We start to realize that fear, depression, and anxiety are gifts given to us on a silver platter because on the other side of all of this is freedom!

Once we truly lean into our fear, it begins to dissolve, and we find ourselves acting from a place of strength and love. As we cultivate gratitude around our fear our life takes on new purpose. This is real courage.

Thank all that is for this moment...

WE ARE NOT OUR BODY

Spiritual beings having a human experience

Our bodies are part of our outer world. It is common knowledge that there isn't one cell in your entire body that was there seven years ago. By constantly gathering information on how to heal our bodies we often overlook the more important piece of the puzzle. Worry is the enemy, not our bodies!

The mind controls the body. This means in essence, that our mind is our body. As we de-stress the mind, the body will naturally heal. One of the deepest root stresses in our collective consciousness is that something is wrong with our bodies.

Do you currently have an underlying thought stream that tells you that something is wrong with your body? Really think about it for a second, and be brutally honest with yourself.

Do you wish your body to be different in any way? Either from a health perspective, or an appearance perspective.

Most of us don't accept our bodies exactly as they are. Our internal dialog goes something like this: If only I could lose some weight. If only I were taller. If only I felt better. If only I didn't have pain in my lower back. If only I had time to exorcise more. If only I had the discipline to do yoga. If only I could change my eating habits. **THIS LIST NEVER ENDS!**

Imagine seven billion people on earth having thoughts like these throughout their day. This is the problem, not our bodies! We create our own health issues.

What we are telling ourselves about our bodies is literally killing us. This is merely the human ego's attempt at avoiding death, and looking good in the process! Nothing more. When we believe the stories in our minds, our body will always be a source of conflict. We may even get a perfect score on our doctor's visits. We make look so young, vibrant and beautiful, that we are the envy of all of the land. We will continue to suffer, until we drop all judgement around our body.

Let's look at this from another perspective. Any conflict we have around our body is causing stress. Stress is the very thing that is aging us, and robbing us of our innate ability to properly care for our body.

We may have always thought that if we could influence the health and appearance of our body through will power, the stress would go away. When this didn't work we became even more stressed out.

We may have gotten so used to this stress, we didn't even know it was there. Ultimately, this stress will be the demise of our body.

By eliminating the root cause of all of our health issues, which is stress, we are able to naturally care for our bodies with little effort. No more crazy diets. No more killing yourself with excessive exercise. Simply going with the flow of life. This is the science of Yoga at work!

Once the stress is removed from our body we find ourselves eating exactly what your body needs. We also find ourselves taking in the right amount of exercise well. We don't even have to think about it.

Thank the energy of love for this moment...

THE DREAM

Can you prove that any of this is real? It can't be proved that I exist, you exist or the universe either. It could all be a dream.

It would be impossible to prove otherwise. This concept can be somewhat comforting when we get really stressed out about something.

No matter what we think is happening it is simply our perception. Everything in our so called universe that we can see touch or feel, has shifted in form as soon as it is perceived.

Nothing has meaning until our thinking mind assigns meaning to it. Nothing! We don't actually exist, until we think we do!

We create our own suffering

If you were a being from outer space looking at the earth from a great distance away though a telescope you would see quite a bit of activity. Some of the movement would be weather related, some would be the animals on land or sea, and some would be human activity.

Humans might not be perceived much differently than any of the other movement on earth. We would simply be observed as something else moving around on that planet.

Everything on earth is in motion all of the time, just as earth itself is in motion all of the time. An alien from outer space may not understand any reason for us to be fighting with each other.

When we cultivate a life of love and stillness, we become aware that nothing is really going on. We realize that we are creating our own little drama. When nothing is going on we don't have anything to react to. It's beautiful!

Consider this. If everyone on our tiny planet adopted this perspective about everything, there would be no more war or fighting. Media conglomerates do not want us to think like this. We might not tune in anymore!

Life is like a movie. The average life expectancy for a human is approximately eighty years these days. So this is like an eighty year movie! We get to sit back, eat some popcorn, and enjoy the show!

Thank the stillness for this moment...

THE MECHANICS OF CREATING

Heaven on earth

True creation manifest from absolutely nothing. There is no evidence or preconceived idea that it could have occurred. It feels magical when this happens but it is not. It is merely natural law.

The ability to create happens when we are able to access the moment, and let go of everything in our mind completely. Allowing all thoughts of doubt, worry, or indecision to be observed as merely thoughts, not realities.

The first and most powerful method of creating is through letting go and surrendering completely to source, or God. This means letting go of all ideas we have for our present moment, and future.

By focusing on the energy of love we have no preconceived ideas, goals or aspirations. We are a blank canvas, wide open to possibilities. We are totally free.

This can be blissful but not always. At this level of awareness there is no desire because we are experiencing sense of total oneness. In my experience, what has appeared in my life from a place of total surrender, has been mind boggling, completely unpredictable, and far exceeded my wildest dreams. This requires full trust.

The second type of creating is from intention. This is very powerful as well. The difference here is that you have a possible outcome or expectation attached to your creation.

In this type of creating you will set an intention to accomplish something. The intention must be in line with your heart's desire for it to manifest.

Let's say you want to write a script for a play. First you must go into your heart and identify the message you would like to portray. You would then set an intention from your heart to pass this particular message on to the audience.

You would visualize an audience member truly feeling this message. You will actually feel in that moment what the audience member will feel when they see your play.

This intention comes from the love that exist within you. The universe will always support any intention from your heart. The next step is to completely get present, and let go of any outcomes associated with your play.

Allow the energy to flow through you in that moment. Then you wait and do nothing. What will happen next is amazing. As soon as you let go and wait, the words for your script will literally be channeling through you from the source of everything.

This is the energy of love flowing through you. This energy has the capacity to tap in to all of your intelligence, empathy, sense of humor, and irony at the same time with zero effort!

This is how we create through intention. The intention of the human heart always has the power of the universe behind it. This requires trust. Letting go of the outcome in any situation is paramount.

No expectations. Remember we are dealing with energy. An expectation of any kind is always fear based. When we mix fear into a creative process we block the energy.

We can create anything we want or need using the methods above. The universe literally has our back at all times. We need only float down-stream and allow the mystery to unfold. Our next moment is unknown. The unknown is what makes life so interesting.

Thank you for this moment – exactly as it is

SYNCHRONICITY

Have you ever been thinking about someone, and your phone rang and it was them? Remember a time when you needed money for something important, and it simply fell into your lap from an unexpected source? We have all had these experiences.

The answers to all of life's questions are right in front of us. Below is a breakdown of the third, fourth, and fifth dimensions of consciousness.

Keep in mind that in the fourth and fifth dimensions we are unblocked from our higher self, and we experience synchronicity more frequently.

Third dimension

Known as the waking state of consciousness. 3D is a very dense, ego based, existence. This is the plane of the material world. Most people on earth today are entirely invested in the third dimension.

Examples of the third dimension are: Over-thinking; Constant planning; Weighing the pros and cons; Figuring things out; Being sarcastic; Being critical of self and others; Gossiping; Hanging on to old ideas and beliefs; identification with the body; overly competitive; Constantly thinking about the past or future.

This is hell on earth. Many people have gotten so accustomed to living this way they don't even know it. They are desensitized.

Here are some rationalizations that people in the third dimension will use to defend their position. I am a hard worker. I am a smart person. I am an honest person. I am a good business person. I am a good parent or guardian. I am successful.

Anytime we add something to the words I am, we are limiting ourselves. This is not bad or wrong. There are billions of absolutely beautiful people living this way. It is simply stressful, and it is a choice.

In the third dimension we find limited power to make real changes in our lives. We are not be open to what is right in front of us.

Sometimes it takes a life-altering event or becoming absolutely miserable to shake someone loose from this state of consciousness. But this doesn't have to be the case.

Fourth Dimension

This is where we start to give up control, and embrace uncertainty. We begin to become aware that we are an infinite source of energy, temporarily in a human body. We rise above our thinking and emotions.

We are less interested in controlling our life, and more interested in allowing it to unfold naturally. We start to become more interested in what we offer to others. We stop keeping track of what we have done for others and we are grateful.

We are not interested in the illusion of financial security, we have an inner knowing that all has been taken care of.

We notice abundance in our lives in all circumstances, realizing that abundance occurs from the inside first then the outside. We seldom feel desperate or insecure. We are open to all possibilities, with no comparing, labeling or judging.

We create holistic relationships that nurture our soul. We begin to live in the moment, and really enjoy our life. We are seldom concerned with how we appear to others.

We are able to laugh at ourselves, and not take life too seriously. We create beautiful, and seemingly impossible gifts in our lives. All of this occurs with very little effort. In the fourth dimension we are starting to live from our heart not our rational thinking mind.

Fifth Dimension

In the fifth dimension of consciousness we are still occupying the same physical space as those in the third and fourth dimensions, but we may as well be on a different planet.

What is true for someone experiencing the fifth dimension would be labelled as absurd by someone in the third dimension. All barriers to peace and love dissolve.

On this plane life becomes fairy tale like. Food taste better. Colors are brighter and more vibrant. We love everything and everyone unconditionally.

We never become needy or overly attached to anything. We are able to create anything we need immediately.

We are only interested in raising human consciousness through any means necessary. We are seldom worried about anyone or anything.

We see all events through the lens of the divine with zero judgement. We live in one hundred percent surrender to the moment, and our heart.

All of our relationships become holistic in nature. Meaning our only purpose to be in any relationship is to help each other grow spiritually. We see everything as a lesson.

Life on earth is temporary. We know that we are here at this time to assist others, and for no other reason.

We aren't impressed with anything humans have accomplished or ever will accomplish. We have accessed the power of love. Life can still be uncomfortable at times but we embrace this gracefully.

When we begin to reach the fourth and fifth levels of consciousness, we see synchronicity all around us. All day every day we notice seemingly magical occurrences.

We are not be blocked from walking through the doors that open. It becomes normal for us to do this. We make choices in our life that seem insane to others because they are not based in physical facts. Our choices are based on trust, and intuition.

In the fourth and fifth dimension's nothing on the outside defines us. The health and appearance of our body are secondary to what is really important, our soul and spirit. It is extremely important not to become attached to any state of mind because whatever you are experiencing now will change.

Thank the grace of God for this moment...

THE CURRENCY OF LOVE

Love, not money, is the ultimate currency of life. It is always easier to ask for money, or part with money when we perceive that it's for a good cause. This is the energy of love at work.

In these cases we have chosen to trust that intentions are pure, therefore we are justified in asking for or parting with money. What if every financial transaction in our lives were this easy?

Most of society is operating from a mindset of lack. This is simply fear about not having our wants and needs met, and often blaming others for our dilemma. Many of our wealthiest people live their lives from this perspective.

It is possible to completely reverse this mindset in our own life. As we begin to clear the stress out of our minds and body, we are left with only love in our heart.

From this mindset money comes easily to us, with very little effort. We are no longer blocked or getting our own way. By clearing away all of the confusion, we intuitively know how we can serve our fellow man, and be well compensated for it. We will be operating from a place of giving and serving.

The only real reason for receiving money is to eventually share it with others. This is what makes the world go around. When we attempt to block the flow of money due to selfishness, greed, or fear of lack, everyone suffers.

Once we shift our perspective we part with our money freely, knowing that it is an expression of love. Our wants and needs become one.

We can achieve an inner balance where we seldom want anything we don't actually need. Therefore we always remain in a positive flow financially.

Living this way is the same as being financially independent or wealthy. All needs are met, and all debts are satisfied with little effort or worry. This way of life is real, and available to everyone.

We can literally change the world one person at a time by shifting our actions from fear to love. As we do this many of our social issues will begin to dissipate.

It takes courage and consistency to make this shift. Once we start living from this perspective we often find out that there are many others already living this way. Love spreads very quickly!

Thank God for this moment – exactly as it is

DOMINO EFFECT

We are seldom doing something for the reason we think we are. As we travel through our day, we are constantly sharing our energy with everyone around us. We can alter someone's life without realizing it.

Let's imagine that five years ago you decided to go on a vacation to Alaska for a week. Having never been to Alaska you became focused on what you would do while you were there, and what you would wear.

When you got there you busied yourself with activities such as hiking, fishing, and sight-seeing. This was very fulfilling and exciting. It served as a break from your everyday life.

When it was time to leave you took a mental inventory of your trip. You thought to yourself, "what a great trip I really enjoyed myself".

You may not even remember a brief exchange with a local lady sitting next to you at a coffee shop, the second day you were there. She had noticed that you turned your cellphone off, closed your eyes for five minutes, and ignored everything going on around you.

After you opened your eyes she politely asked you why you had your eyes closed. You replied that you were focusing on gratitude for a few minutes.

Later that day, the lady became aware that something was missing in her life. She got on the internet and found a meditation teacher, and began her inner journey.

Six months later she is happier than she has ever been, and is sharing her new found peace with her entire community.

So in essence the 30 second exchange that you don't even remember, with someone you didn't know, affected many lives for years to come. Maybe this is why you went to Alaska!

Thank the stillness for this moment...

COLLECTIVE INSANITY

We are one being...

The collective insanity of the human mind is our only societal problem. All of our dysfunction comes from our collective ego. Not some of it, all of it.

Here is a list of issues that the human ego is causing. Poverty, Terrorism, Racism, Religious disputes, Obesity, Addiction, Pollution, Crime, and every other perceived problem we have.

Ask yourself this question. Who do we think we are? Are we no better than a selfish child screaming uncontrollably for a new toy, when he has a pile of unused toys right in front of him. Think about it for a second.

We tend to point the finger at everyone else. This is judgement, which is the greatest separator of all. We are all in on this together. We are simply misinformed as to how to solve these issues.

It starts in a seemingly small way, with you and me.

We have the power to change the world in this very moment by tapping into our natural state of love. Our love will spread to others like a wildfire on a dry windy day.

It is such a relief when we can simply let go. When we let go of worrying about anything, we realize that we really are ok right now.

What if everyone on earth let go at the same time. This is what we need to focus on. It is the only thing we need to be focusing on.

This may seem over simplistic, but aren't the best things in life simple? A great song, your mothers apple pie, two children laughing in the park, puppy dog eyes, or a volleyball game at the beach on a hot summer day. Let's get back to living simply.

By letting go of that which is blocking us from being truly connected, we will return to a life of love and simplicity. An easy shift from constant doing to simply being.

Thank all that is for this moment...

OUR HIGHEST CALLING

Everything that has been discussed in this book points towards enlightenment. This enables us to "Just be", and allow our lives to unfold naturally, and effortlessly.

By accomplishing this we automatically elevate every living creature on earth. This is the energy of love.

When are able to slow down and surrender thoughts, deeds, and actions to our higher self, we are naturally more available to help those in need. Our energy alone will attract opportunities to serve that may have existed, but we wouldn't have noticed them.

Getting out of ourselves and helping others, expecting nothing in return, is its own reward. This is why we are here.

We are living in an extremely exciting time! The world is experiencing a major shift. The energy of love is gaining momentum every day in the face of extreme chaos.

Our highest calling is to raise our own vibration of love and appreciate the moment. In doing so we energetically help others do the same. We can all make a difference one person at a time.

Thank the stillness for this moment….

Part 2
Practices

AWARENESS

Remember a time when you suddenly knew everything about something, but you had no idea how you gained this knowledge? Have you ever been on a quiet beach, and became overwhelmed with peace and joy for no reason.

These are brief states of pure awareness filled with gratitude and knowing. While we are in this state we actually know everything we will ever need to know in the moment.

Awareness is the ability to absorb everything that is happening in the universe at once. Observing from a place of stillness. Full understanding of the how and why of everything, without questioning, or attempting to explain.

We can tap into a knowing that is far beyond the scope of whatever we are paying attention to in any given moment. We can retrain our minds to allow our intuition to be the dominant player in our decision making. When we are constantly paying attention to our thoughts and being outwardly distracted, we are blocking the flow of love from within.

Awareness is a much higher form of intelligence. When we are truly aware in the moment, we are in a state of being. We can remain in a state of being, and at the same time be extremely active.

Awareness is a place of observation, void of desire in the moment. As we begin to observe our thoughts from a distance, we create space or gaps in our thinking. We can then stop identifying with the negative, and confusing chatter oc-curring in our mind.

The moment we start watching our thoughts, a higher level of consciousness becomes activated. We begin to realize that there is a mountain of intelligence beyond thought, and that thought is only a fraction of that intelligence.

We begin to realize what truly matters in life – beauty, love, creativity joy, and inner peace.

All of the practices outlined in this book are designed to cultivate awareness. Staring with commitment. Without a strong commitment, and steady practice, there can be little progress.

Thank the energy of love for this moment...

COMMITMENT

One of the most significant blocks to finding personal freedom is lack of commitment. That means is that we are choosing to remain committed to the old way instead of re-directing our commitment to the new way. We are hanging on. This is the opposite of freedom.

Hanging on, in any form, is choosing to remain blocked. This choice isn't good or bad, it is simply a choice.

The simple act of truly committing to something will raise our vibration significantly.

There are several extremely effective practices outlined in the remainder of this book. These simple practices are specifi-cally aimed at helping us cultivate awareness. This may be the most difficult journey of your life but it will also be the most rewarding. Once you begin to experience freedom you will never go back to your previous ways.

As we commit these practices will become automatic. As this way of life becomes a habit, we will energetically attract new practices to take us further and further.

Thank the grace of God for this moment...

RIGHT BRAIN-LEFT BRAIN

For eons we have relied on the left or analytical side of our brain to meet all of our needs including those of a spiritual nature.

Examples of this are; Gathering information from religious text or spiritually based books. Listening to the spoken word of a preacher, Rabbi or spiritual guru. Attending uplifting positive seminars focused on realizing our potential. All of these practices are fantastic and will improve your life, but there is so much more!

The following practices are designed to go beneath the surface of the mind and dissolve stress and ignorance from its root. They will also tap you into the female or creative side of your mind, while continuing to satisfy the left brain. This will create balance.

These practices have nothing to do with gathering information or believing anything. These are mechanical processes designed to get us out of our head, and into our heart.

The only rule to any of these practices is that we DO NOT TRY. Simply allow them to unfold naturally and be extremely gentle with yourself.

Thank the universe for this moment...

QUIET OBSERVATION

When we are continually focused outwardly we are blocking the love from within from expressing itself. The natural tendency of our mind is to move inward toward peace and joy.

This is the practice of observing your thoughts and feeling your feelings. This practice is extremely powerful as it begins to dissolve lifelong stress from the root so that it never returns.

You will begin to rise above your thinking and see things clearly. You can practice this with your eyes closed or throughout your day with your eyes open. It is most powerful when you do both.

The benefits of this are amazing. In a very short period of time you begin to experience a level of peace that words cannot describe. You will begin to purify your thinking.

Practice every day for six weeks and evaluate where you are. You must commit. You will raise your vibration significantly by simply committing. You will be accessing the energy of gratitude as you practice.

Instruction

1. Sit or lay very comfortably anywhere you choose, and close your eyes.

2. Think to yourself "thank you for this moment – exactly as it is". The word "you" in the phrase is place holder

for whatever you call your highest force for good. Examples are God, the universe, nature, spirit, and so on. There is immense power in this phrase. Do not focus on your breath. If you have been trained to focus on your breath from yoga or other meditations, let that habit go for this practice only. Breathe normally.

3. After you think the phrase let it go, and begin to watch your thoughts and notice your feelings. DO NOT attempt to block your thoughts or feelings, this will block the energy flow.

4. After some time passes think "thank you for this moment- exactly as it is" again. Always allow your intuition to guide you as to when to think the technique again. Do not repeat the technique over and over with no time in between. Allow for space.

5. Repeat this process for 20 or 30 minutes twice a day. Morning and evening is best. It's ok to start with 5 or 10 minutes and gradually increase your time every few days. it helps to peak at a clock in the beginning. Eventually your inner clock will kick in.

6. Do not judge your experience. This process will work whether you believe it or not. If you find yourself thinking many thoughts, GREAT! Stress will leave your body as you are thinking. If you have strong feelings pleasant or unpleasant, this is ok.

7. Feel your feelings and allow them to pass. You may also fall into a trance or have very few thoughts. These are all merely experiences and they mean nothing.

8. You cannot do this wrong. Never beat yourself up.
    Just think the technique, let it go, and watch the
    movie pass before the screen. Repeat!

9. When you are finished open your eyes and sit in quiet
    contemplation for a few minutes. This is very relaxing.

As you practice this technique it will take you beneath the
surface of the mind and into your heart. It is not necessary
that you feel grateful as you practice. In fact, you may feel
anything but grateful! You may experience a moment of spacious awareness but if you don't the meditation is still working so do not stop.

Using the technique eyes closed for 30 minutes it is the
equivalent of getting several hours of sleep. So you can re-
charge very quickly.

The more you do this the more benefit you will receive.
By closing your eyes two times a day for 30 minutes each you
will begin to dissolve lifelong impressions.

This practice may bring up old stuff that has been sup-
pressed in your subconscious from the past. This may be
uncomfortable but stay the course. There is a light at the end
of the tunnel.

Stress will exit your body as you think. DO NOT TRY
TO BLOCK YOUR THOUGHTS. ALLOW THEM TO
FLOW NATURALLY. SIMPLY OBSERVE THEM.

Thank you for this moment – exactly as it is

NOTICE AND CHOOSE

Eyes open throughout the day

Thoughts are not reality. They simply come and go naturally. Some are pleasurable some aren't. The same can be said about feelings. They are merely energy moving and always changing. The idea is to focus on what never changes, which is the energy of creation.

As we go about our day, anytime we notice a thought or feeling we think the phrase **"thank you for this moment – exactly as it is"**. This is equally as important as the eyes closed method.

Non-judgement- Anytime we notice our mind judging anything, especially ourselves or anyone else, we effortlessly think the phrase.

Non-stealing- This can be as simple as focusing on the negative. When we do this we rob ourselves from the love that exist within. In turn we rob everyone else of love as well. Think the phrase "thank you for this moment", and let it go.

Non-grasping- Anytime we notice ourselves wanting anything for fear- based reasons we are grasping. For instance if we want a nicer home so that we will receive approval from our peers we are grasping. There isn't anything wrong with wanting things. We find peace when we are honest about why we want them. Think the phrase in this moment.

Non-violence- When we are thinking thoughts of re-
venge or jealousy we think the phrase. Thinking the phrase in
these moments will bring compassion into our heart.

Truthfulness- This applies when we aren't honest about
something. Especially our feelings. We think the phrase in
this situation.

If we feel stress because we are late for something, we think
the phrase. If we have a warm and fuzzy thought about our
dog, we think the phrase. This will begin to train your mind to
not make giant distinctions between pleasant and unpleasant
activity. Eventually everything starts to be more pleasurable.

Try it at work, driving, practicing yoga, working out, or taking
a long mindful walk. No matter what you are doing the technique
will bring you back to gratitude and acceptance in the moment.

As you practice this technique it will take you beneath the
surface of the mind and into your heart. You will actually make
contact with source every time you think the phrase. Remember
you are saying "thank you" to your higher self or God.

By choosing to think the phrase all day with your eyes
open, you will prevent new stress from occurring. Eventually
you will anchor a sense of peace and well-being.

Every time you create a moment of non-thinking awareness you are experiencing the energy of God or source. You
are tapped into a higher frequency immediately. The key is to
bring yourself back to this experience as often as possible.

Thank the source of everything for this moment...

APPRECIATION, GRATITUDE, LOVE

Notice and choose

Every time we notice a thought, feeling or concept we can choose for appreciation, gratitude, and love throughout our day. This is an effortless way to rise above out thoughts, feelings and limiting beliefs.

Appreciation

Practice actively appreciating your life, as it is, in this moment.

Gratitude

Say thank you to God or the universe all day for things big and small. Think "thank you" when someone cuts you off in traffic this may even make you laugh. Think "thank you "when you are irritated with someone and the irritation will eventually dissolve.

If you have a negative thought about your body focus on gratitude. As you focus on gratitude your stress and fear around your body will dissipate.

As you practice this diligently you will create neuropathways in your mind to have an automatic response of gratitude. This is both scientific and spiritual. It will alter reality very quickly.

Before you know it by practicing gratitude you will find yourself laughing at little things. Few things will disturb you as before and you will have joy in your life.

As you think "thank you" to God or source all day every-day your external circumstances begin to shift in your favor as well. This feels like magic but it's not. Gratitude is one of the highest frequencies available to us.

With gratitude you access the power to alter anything in your life with little effort. The law of attraction will kick in very quickly.

Love

Love is the most powerful force in the universe. Nothing can compete with the benevolent force of real love. As we fill our consciousness with more love we simultaneously reduce fear.

Think the phrase 'I love you" throughout your day. Place your awareness on your heart as you do this. Remember this is God or source telling you how much you are loved. The more awkward this is, the more you need it.

Thank nature for this moment…

THE PRACTICE OF
FORGIVENESS

All is forgiven

Close your eyes for 10 to 20 minutes and place your awareness on your heart. Then think the words, "I forgive you". You are imagining God or the universe whispering these words to you. Then feel your feelings and observe your thoughts....

Allow for space

Then with your eyes still closed listen to the soft voice of God or the universe whispering "I forgive you" to someone you are angry or mildly at odds with or resent. Feel your feelings and observe your thoughts...

Allow for space

With your eyes still closed listen to the melodic voice of God or source whispering "I forgive you" to everyone on earth past and present. Feel your feelings, observe your thoughts... repeat.

As we forgive ourselves we dissolve shame. When we forgive others we are no longer playing the victim. When we forgive the world at large we are healing our false belief in separation. There really isn't anything wrong. Everything is perception.

Thank the energy of love for this moment...

THE PRACTICE OF COMPASSION

Compassion often looks and feels like the opposite

True compassion comes from the ability to see ourselves, without judgement, in everyone no matter how opposite to us they may appear. This is a heart to heart connection that allows us to be gentle, loving, and kind. This isn't possible if we are always in a hurry or self-absorbed.

Being ruthlessly compassionate with someone is doing what is in someone's best interest without compromising yourself. This can be an empathetic gesture, refusal to enable someone, or not doing anything. Compassion is a combination of empathy and the wisdom not to harm ourself in the process.

It is impossible to have true compassion for others if we don't have it for ourselves first. If we are running around trying to save the world, it is likely that we have guilt or self-judgement. This is the opposite of compassion.

Think the word compassion periodically throughout the day, especially if you are being angry, or judgmental. Remember you must be compassionate toward yourself first in order to truly impact others.

There is light in everyone and everything. It is our privilege to find the light in everyone and help them to see what we see.

Thank the universe for this moment...

THE PRACTICE OF ACCEPTANCE

Think the phrase "thank you for this moment" and now add the words "exactly as it is". This will tap you into radical acceptance quickly. So all day long think "thank you for this moment-exactly as it is".

Being at odds with what is, is at the root of most human suffering. There can be no peace or true happiness until we begin to accept everything exactly as it is.

Our thinking mind is incapable of full acceptance. The ego is merely a built-in tool we have to aid with our basic survival needs. It is only capable of labeling, judging, comparing, rationalizing, gathering information, and attempting to control outcomes.

There is absolutely zero capacity to fully accept anything in this part of our mind. We may be able to temporarily alter our behavior through an intellectual understanding of acceptance, but this will be fleeting at best.

Be open to the lesson of everything! We are connected to everything. When we are dissatisfied with anything, we are ultimately dissatisfied with ourselves.

There is a tremendous sense of relief and freedom when we choose to accept life as it is. We may still become upset at times but it won't last long.

Thank God for this moment-exactly as it is

THE PRACTICE OF TRUST

In order to fully trust we must let go of the past, and all expectation of the future. We need only trust the source within. Everything else will fall into place. Our choice.

This doesn't mean we turn a blind eye, and simply trust everyone implicitly. Quite the opposite. Ignoring our intuition leads to an overall distrust of everything and everyone.

Intuition never lies

When we feel a slight restriction in our chest it is trying to tell us something. If we go against this divine advice, we are either imbalanced, and or confused.

If our mind is running a hundred miles an hour we may not notice our chest tightening, which leads to more confusion.

Through the practice of choosing appreciation, gratitude and love we can strip away all of the anxiety around trust. When we begin to love ourselves, we don't need to trust some-one else to love us. We can fully trust our inner voice.

Thank the stillness for this moment...

THE PRACTICE OF
ALLOWING

Become more efficient with far less effort

Letting go of the attachment to any outcome is allowing. Giving up perceived control is allowing.

You may have a strong perception about something causing you to want to take a certain action. This is reacting to life. There is little power when we react.

By feeling our feelings fully and allowing them to pass, our intuition will becomes very noticeable. Maybe we do nothing instead of reacting. Maybe we just wait. When we live this way you will begin to notice that we are always in a natural flow. No confusion.

All feelings originate with thought. We first have a thought or perception. Then we have a feeling around that thought. If we react to that thought we are not allowing.

Everything in life is temporary and always in motion. Allowing life to unfold naturally causes everything to slow down and make sense. Situations that used to feel overwhelming become easy.

A difficult relationship can shift quickly. Health issues subside. Productivity increases. Creativity is enhanced. You are actually allowing love to flow through you. No more pressure.

Thank the divine for this moment...

TOTAL SURRENDER

The practice of...

A wise man once said that surrender is the door to everything. The energy of creation is everything, everywhere, and in every moment. Surrendering our thoughts, feelings, deeds and actions to God or Source on the outside, and on the inside, is our only path to self-realization. This is an egoless existence. But how can we do this?

Through the power of choice

This isn't difficult. Anytime we choose to turn the gaze away from our perceived problems and directly at the energy of love, we are surrendered. In that moment we aren't trying to receive anything, even peace of mind. We are embracing total uncertainty with our heart wide open to whatever comes next. Even if it isn't what we wanted. Knowing that all is correct in spite of the fact that we may be experiencing great discomfort.

Once we fully surrender in any given moment we are graced with our natural state of divine love. From this beautiful place we are able to love ourselves completely and be of true service to others.

A perfect way to practice this is to effortlessly think the Sanskrit words **"Om Namah Shivaya"** throughout the day. This means "thy will be done" or "surrender to the one."

Om Namah Shivaya is a statement of pure love and will surgically penetrate the dense ego mind. Sanskrit is a living language so as you think these words you are simultaneously invoking the meaning behind them. If you do not feel comfortable using the Sanskrit phrase simply think "**Thy will be done**". The human ego will never utter these words and will find them repulsive. Even more reason to think them!

By alternating the phrases "**Thank you for this moment – exactly as it is,**" and "**Thy will be done,**" throughout our day with our eyes open, and with our eyes closed as a meditation three times a day, we begin to experience surrender.

It is possible to act our way into better thinking temporarily. Long term if we attempt to surrender through changing our behavior or reorganizing our outer world, without first addressing our thinking mind, we will have little success and inevitably become frustrated. When we address our mind first and become heart centered, our outer world follows nicely.

The ego can never surrender. However through our power of choice we can fully surrender by focusing on gratitude, love, and compassion in every moment. This is simple math. We merely choose a thought based in love, directly into thousands of fear based thoughts, and we create a tipping point where love becomes the new operating system for our life. What we focus on grows! When we are surrendered, we are in a flow state like a flock of birds flying in perfect formation. We are simply being.

In my own life, I vow on a daily basis to surrender what is left of myself or my ego to the energy of creation which I call love. This is a choice to remain in the eye of the storm and to always flow downstream with whatever life presents. Like my mother used to say when I was a small child, "I wouldn't trade this way of life for all the tea in China!"

Om Namah Shivaya

ADDITIONAL PRACTICES

Below are some additional practices you may want to experiment with. Some of these may seem a bit odd but that is the point. Take what you want and leave the rest!

- Yoga, Yoga, Yoga!   (remember it's not a competition)

- Get out into nature. Appreciate the sun, moon, and stars. Gratitude for the rain, snow, wind, and sleet. Love for the plants, animals, and sea creatures. Walk barefoot and feel the dirt, grass or sand beneath your feet.

- Take a long walk alone several times a week without your phone or music. Feel every step and listen to the birds. The sound of birds chirping can actually heal you. Breathe deeply as you walk.

- Give money to random strangers from time to time, especially if you don't think you have enough for yourself. Never ask the person what they intend to do with the money.

- Occasionally spend time in public not looking your best. Don't wear your make-up, jewelry, watch, or nice shoes.

    Wear some old sweats. Make zero effort to look a certain way. This is the practice of self-acceptance.

123

- Don't look at prices or read labels at the supermarket occasionally. Fill your basket with all of your familiar items and head to the checkout counter knowing that all is well. This is the practice of abundance.

- Purposely stand in the longest line at the checkout counter, especially if you are in a hurry or running late. Notice every thought and emotion as you do this. This is the practice of patience, and giving up the illusion of control.

- Practice really listening to others, instead of always thinking of what you are going to say next.

- Let go of any need to be right or prove a point as you speak to people. Remain open. This is the practice of trust, and letting go of control.

- Go an entire day in silence without music, speaking to anyone, getting on the computer, cellphone, or reading anything. "Just be"

- Go an entire day consuming only water or lemon-water. This practice is the practice of detachment.

- When you are in contact with others focus on your heart. Focus on their heart at the same time. This will create a connection between you and them. The results of this can be truly magical.

- Go to a park or the beach. Find an open area and begin to walk 100 steps with your eyes closed. This cultivates Trust.

- Do everything more slowly. Eat slower, walk slower, write slower, and talk more slowly.

- Make sure you are breathing deeply throughout your day

- Simplify your life by purging unwanted items and downsizing

- The next time you are on vacation try going to a place in the middle of nowhere. No television, internet or cellphones. While on this vacation, eat only fruit, vegetables, and lean protein. Drink only tea and water. Spend every day meditating, practicing yoga, taking long walks, and reading something uplifting. Spend most of your time in silence and solitude. This can be life altering.

The idea is to practice things like this until they aren't uncomfortable any more. When this occurs we begin to get out of our head and drop into our heart. Life slows down and we are at peace.

Thank nature for this moment...

EXPANSION AND CONTRACTION

Three steps forward two steps back. A spiritual journey is one of expansion and contraction. Our expansive inner journey is wrought with speed bumps and forks in the road. It is very important to have this awareness so that we do not beat ourselves up when we back pedal a bit.

When you begin to slow down and get fully grounded in your heart, you may have extreme highs and lows for a while. This will pass.

The stress that you have been carrying around for years needs to express itself in order to move out of your body.

You may find yourself in tears or angry for seemingly no reason. This is all normal and ok. When you know why this is happening it makes it a lot easier.

If you are committed and consistent you will experience profound progress, and long periods of bliss, followed by times of melancholy and disorientation.

Be mindful that you are letting go of everything you have been holding onto your entire life, because it didn't serve you. You will be grieving the loss of your shadow self.

Once you have cleared the stress out of your system, your expansions will be greater and your contractions smaller. You will be idling at a much higher vibration.

Situations that used to disturb you, will no longer have any impact on you. You're ability to help others will be keener and sharper than ever before.

This is most certainly a journey not a destination. We never arrive, and there is always more. Surrender to your inner self. Thy will be done. May peace and love be with you on your journey!

Thank God for this moment – exactly as it is

PERSONAL TOUCH

It is often said that no-one ever became spiritually enlightened on their own or from reading a book. Of course we are already enlightened from birth but we often need trusted mirrors in our life to reflect the truth when we are off track. It takes a village!

Always think for yourself! There are many valid meditation practices and teachers in the world. It is most important that you trust the person that is teaching you and that they aren't imposing any agenda or belief. It is infinitely more powerful to meditate in a group than alone. The energy is far more intense.

Below are several valid teachings that I have personally practiced and can vouch for. All of these practices ultimately help us to access our heart. It is best if you pick one and stick with it. Trying to practice several things at once can often lead to confusion.

- **The Ishayas' Ascension** is based on the science of union or yoga and it works! Ascension is available worldwide and focuses on creating Christ consciousness through a series of time tested mechanical techniques. Ascension is only taught in person by a qualified teacher. This is to preserve the integrity of the teaching. Ascension quickly reduces stress, transcends the thinking mind, and causes high effortless functioning.

- **The Shamballa Path** is also available worldwide. This Buddhist practice focuses on basic goodness of every human heart. The goal is to create an enlightened society one conversation at a time.

- **The violet flame decrees**. This is a meditation practice that focuses on destroying ignorance, eliminating fear, and restoring health. The flame can be used to transcend negativity and discover truth. Teachers are available.

- **A Course in Miracles.** The study of this text, alongside focused meditation, with an enlightened instructor can be life changing.

- **Zen Meditation.** Focuses on bringing the mind back to the breath and tapping into the in the clarity of here and now. Available worldwide.

- **Contemplative prayer.** This is a meditation focusing on bringing the mind back the experience of God. Teachers and teachings are available.

- **Breathwork and Rebirthing.** These extremely powerful practices aim to heal past traumas and bring fourth an awareness of love in this moment. Teachers are available.

NEVER STOP LAUGHING

We can find humor in any and every situation if we look for it. Being human is downright funny. We really never know what's coming next! If we take it all too seriously, we miss out on the best part of living.

We need to chill out and get over ourselves!

Humor is also very effective in preventing ourselves from becoming arrogant. Great comedians turn out to be some of the most spiritual people around.

They usually come from a traumatic childhood, and through humor, they learn a very detached perspective that makes us laugh. It's beautiful!

Humility and an ability to laugh at ourselves go hand in hand. Why do we have the ability to laugh? I am certainly not interested in knowing the answer to that question. I'm just glad we do.

Thank you for your practice!

FREEDOM

An unencumbered moment, where our attention is not captured by worry or constant chatter, is a moment of freedom. We have an innate ability to observe our own life from a distance with no opinion, as though it were a play.

As we simplify our mind we automatically release unwanted baggage in our outer world. This allows for the love within us to fully shine.

We discover the unlimited splendor of the human experience, and instantly create a new way of living. We gratefully embrace tears of a broken heart, as well as the tears of joy. We perceive everything happening in the world, and our own lives, as a lesson and therefore no big deal. We know that as we stare into the eyes of another, no matter the differences, we are looking in the mirror. In this new way of life we make it our sole purpose to Just Be.

Welcome Home!

Please visit addisonpalmore.com

I would love your feedback…
addison.palmorebe@gmail.com

Feel free to write an honest review…

Made in the USA
Columbia, SC
29 March 2018